Name _____   Date _____

SCHOOL SUPPLIES

Identify the pictures below. Use the word bank below to name each picture.

_____

_____

_____

_____

Word Bank:

| notebook | push pin | book | sharpener |

Name _____ Date _____

SCHOOL SUPPLIES

Identify the pictures below. Use the word bank below to name each picture.

_____
....
_____

_____
....
_____

_____
....
_____

_____
....
_____

Word Bank:

| crayons | scissors | pencil | eraser |

Name _____   Date _____

SCHOOL SUPPLIES

Identify the pictures below. Use the word bank below to name each picture.

_____
....
_____

_____
....
_____

_____
....
_____

_____
....
_____

Word Bank:

| ruler | bag | palette | glue |

Name _____ Date _____

SCHOOL SUPPLIES

Identify the pictures below. Use the word bank below to name each picture.

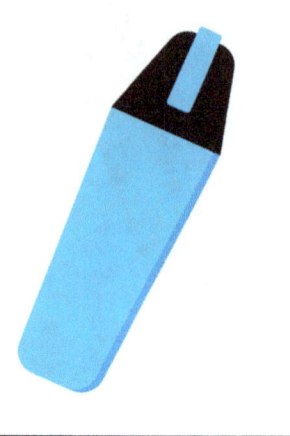

_____
....

_____
....

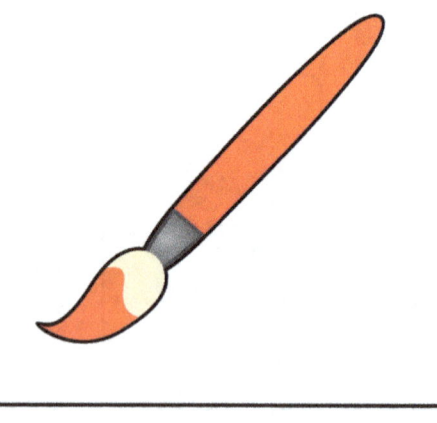

_____
....

_____
....

Word Bank:

| calculator | globe | highlighter | paintbrush |

Name _____   Date _____

SENTENCE WRITING

Look at the picture below. Write a sentence that tells about the picture.

_____
....
_____
_____
....
_____
_____
....
_____

Name _____ Date _____

SENTENCE WRITING

Look at the picture below. Write a sentence that tells about the picture.

Name _____ Date _____

SENTENCE WRITING

Look at the picture below. Write a sentence that tells about the picture.

....
....
....
....
....

Name _____   Date _____

SENTENCE WRITING

Look at the picture below. Write a sentence that tells about the picture.

_____
....
_____
....
_____
....
_____

Name _____   Date _____

SENTENCE WRITING

Look at the picture below. Write a sentence that tells about the picture.

Name _____ Date _____

SENTENCE WRITING

Look at the picture below. Write a sentence that tells about the picture.

Name _____   Date _____

SENTENCE WRITING

Look at the picture below. Write a sentence that tells about the picture.

Name _____   Date _____

MY SCHOOL SUPPLIES

What are the school supplies you have in your bag?

Name _____   Date _____

MY FAVORITE BOOK

What is your favorite book? What is it about?

Name _____   Date _____

COUNTING SCHOOL SUPPLIES

Find and count the following items.

Name _____ Date _____

COUNTING SCHOOL SUPPLIES

Find and count the following items.

Name _____ Date _____

GRAPHING ACTIVITY

Find and graph the items listed. Then answer the questions below.

```
10
 9
 8
 7
 6
 5
 4
 3
 2
 1
```

How many of each?

☐    ☐

☐    ☐

Which item did you find the most of? _____

Which item did you find the least of? _____

Name _____ Date _____

GRAPHING ACTIVITY

Find and graph the items listed. Then answer the questions below.

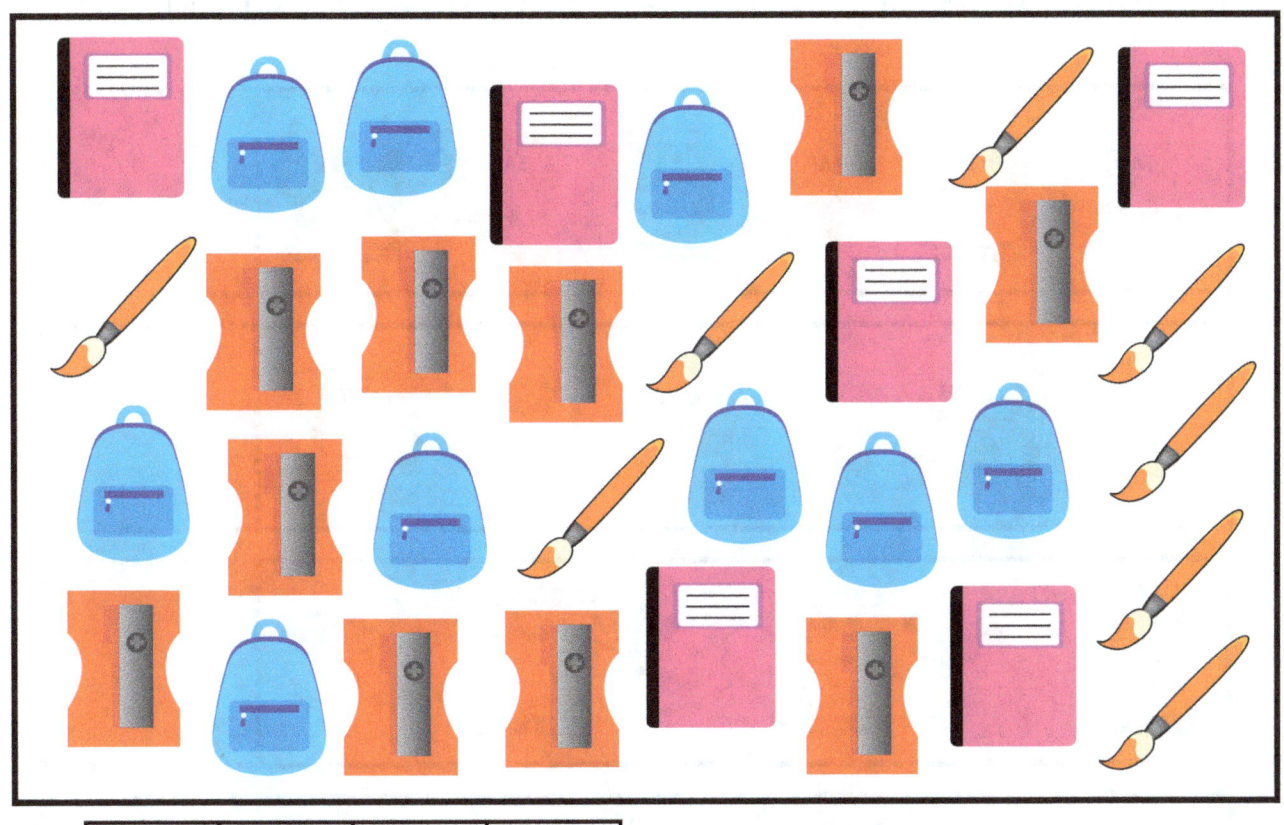

How many of each?

☐ 📓 ☐ 🎒

☐ ✏️ ☐ 🖌️

Which item did you find the most of? _____

Which item did you find the least of? _____

Name ______________________ Date ______________________

FINISH THE PATTERN

Look at the patterns below. Cut out the images at the bottom. Paste the image that comes next in each pattern.

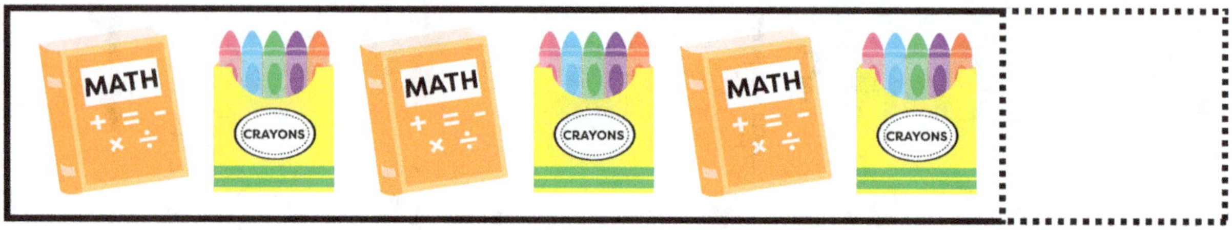

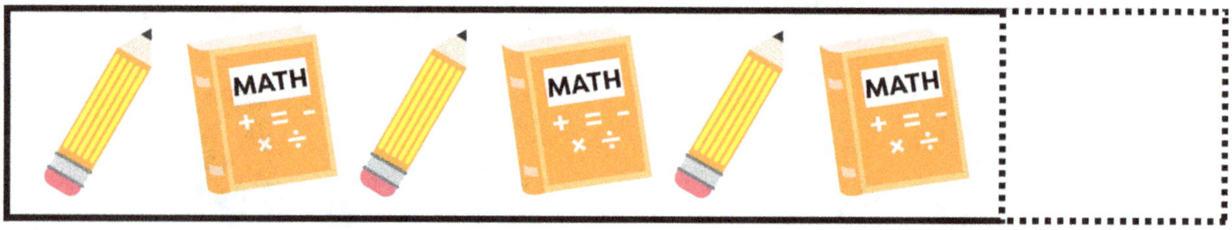

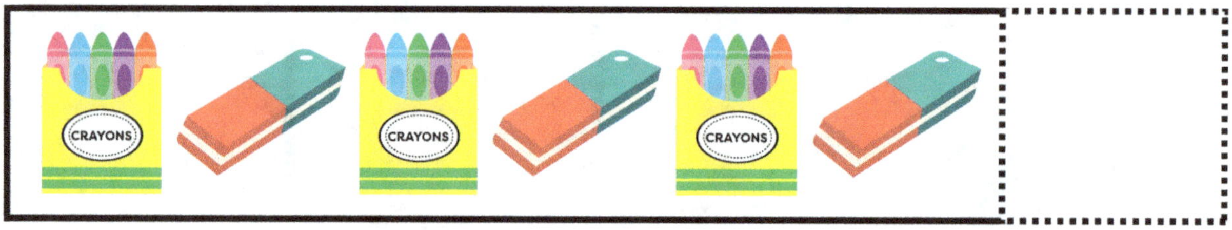

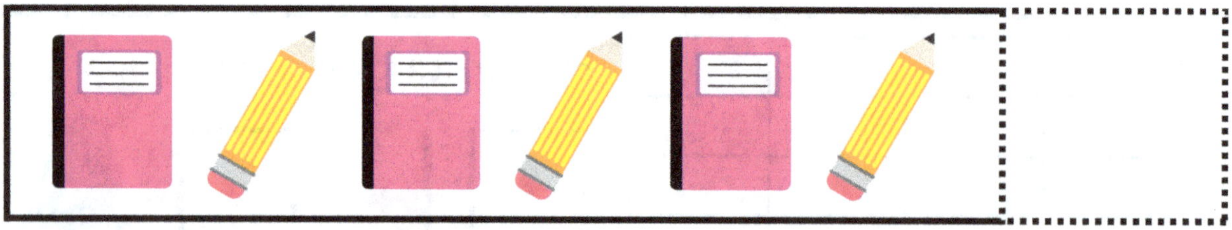

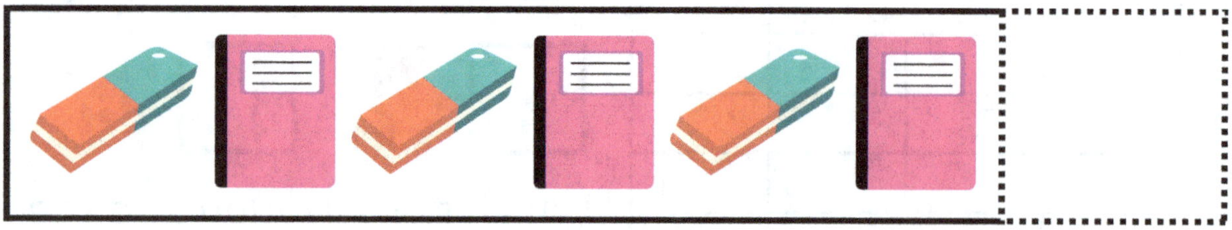

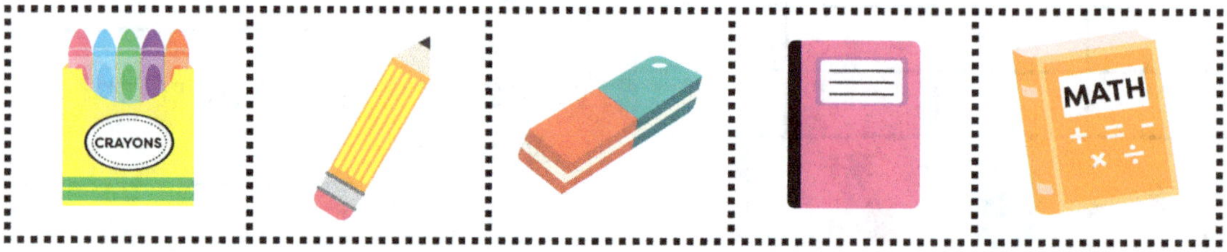

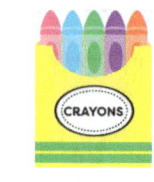

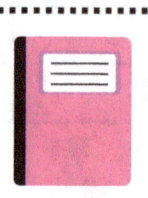

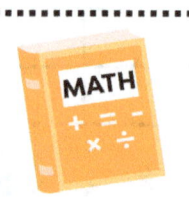

Name _____ Date _____

FINISH THE PATTERN

Look at the patterns below. Cut out the images at the bottom. Paste the image that comes next in each pattern.

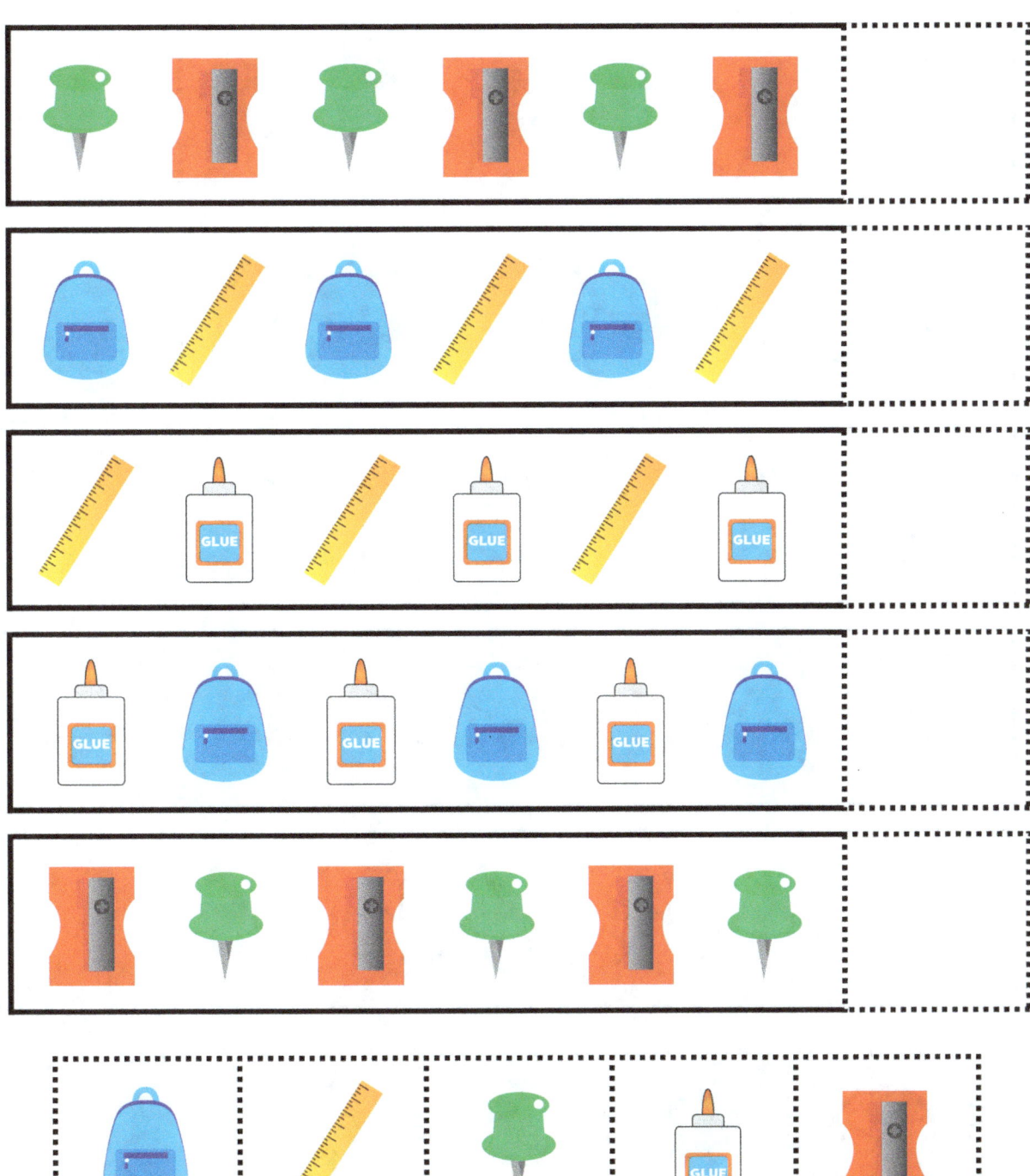

Name _____ Date _____

FINISH THE PATTERN

Look at the patterns below. Cut out the images at the bottom. Paste the image that comes next in each pattern.

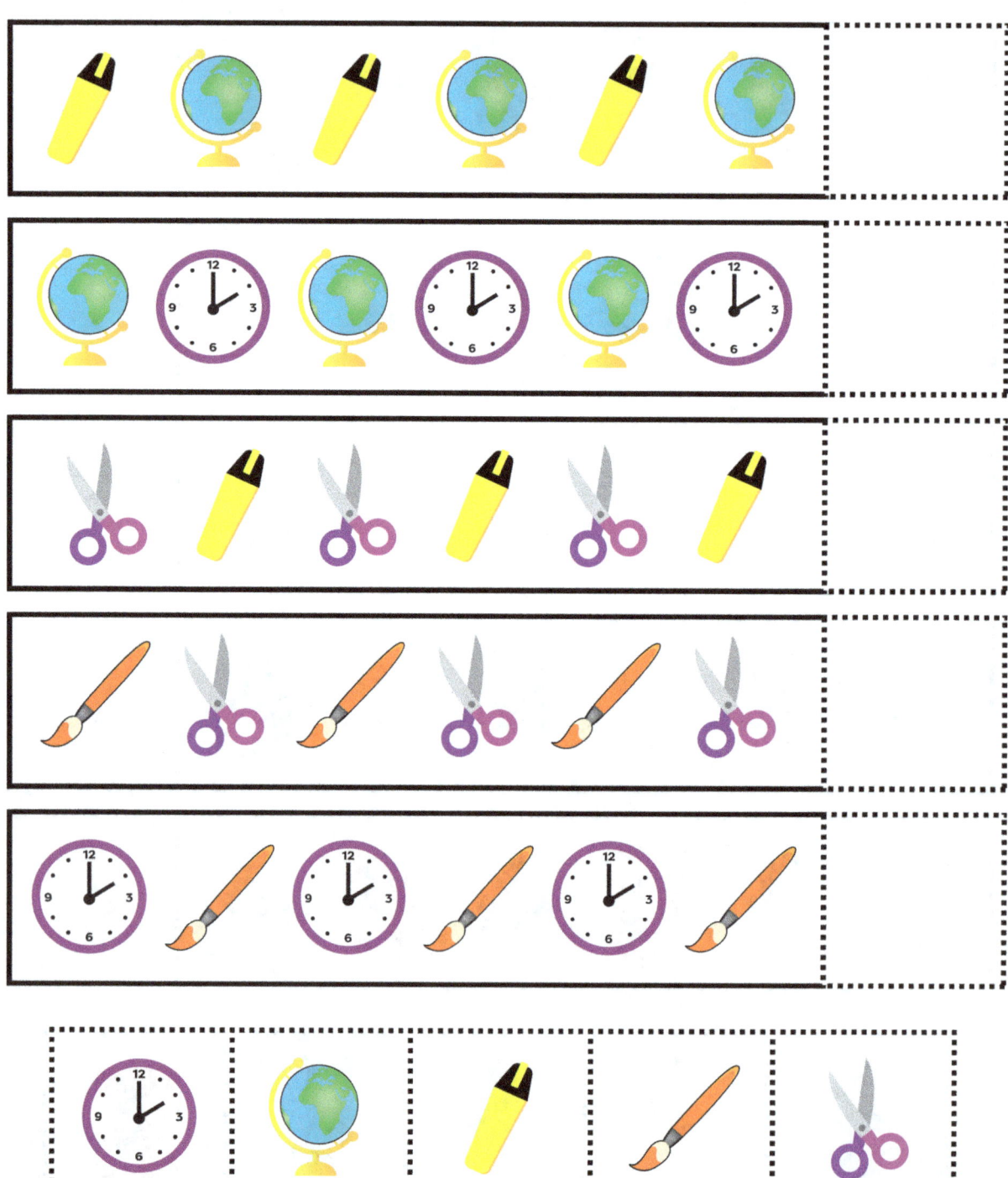

Name _____   Date _____

COLORING ACTIVITY

Color the picture below.

Name _____ Date _____

COLORING ACTIVITY

Color the picture below.

Name _____ Date _____

COLORING ACTIVITY
Color the picture below.

Name _____ Date _____

COLORING ACTIVITY

Color the picture below.

Name _____ Date _____

COLORING ACTIVITY

Color the picture below.

Name _____ Date _____

COLORING ACTIVITY

Color the picture below.

Name _____   Date _____

FAST FOOD

Identify the pictures below. Use the word bank below to name each picture.

_____
....
_____

_____
....
_____

_____
....
_____

_____
....
_____

Word Bank:

| wrap | fries | burger | hotdog |

Name _____   Date _____

FAST FOOD

Identify the pictures below. Use the word bank below to name each picture.

_____
....
_____

_____
....
_____

_____
....
_____

_____
....
_____

Word Bank:

| pizza | salad | popcorn | taco |

Name _____   Date _____

FAST FOOD

Identify the pictures below. Use the word bank below to name each picture.

_____
....
_____

_____
....
_____

_____
....
_____

_____
....
_____

Word Bank:

| noodles | pretzel | cookie | donut |

Name _____ Date _____

FAST FOOD

Identify the pictures below. Use the word bank below to name each picture.

_____

_____

_____

_____

Word Bank:

| ice cream | chips | chocolate | corndog |

Name _____   Date _____

SENTENCE WRITING

Look at the picture below. Write a sentence that tells about the picture.

....
_____
....
_____
....
_____
....
_____

Name _____   Date _____

SENTENCE WRITING

Look at the picture below. Write a sentence that tells about the picture.

Name _____ Date _____

SENTENCE WRITING

Look at the picture below. Write a sentence that tells about the picture.

_____
_____
_____
_____
_____

Name _____   Date _____

SENTENCE WRITING

Look at the picture below. Write a sentence that tells about the picture.

_____
_____
_____
_____
_____

Name _____ Date _____

SENTENCE WRITING

Look at the picture below. Write a sentence that tells about the picture.

....
_____
_____
....
_____
_____
....

Name _____ Date _____

SENTENCE WRITING

Look at the picture below. Write a sentence that tells about the picture.

_____
....
_____
....
_____
....
_____

Name _____ Date _____

SENTENCE WRITING

Look at the picture below. Write a sentence that tells about the picture.

Name _____ Date _____

MY FAVORITE FAST FOOD

What is your favorite fast food?

Name _____ Date _____

MAKING A PIZZA

What are the steps in making a pizza?

Name _____   Date _____

COUNTING ACTIVITY

Find and count the following items.

  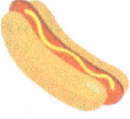  

Name _____ Date _____

COUNTING ACTIVITY

Find and count the following items.

Name _____   Date _____

GRAPHING ACTIVITY

Find and graph the items listed. Then answer the questions below.

How many of each?

☐ 🍪   ☐ 🌮

☐ 🍫   ☐ 🌭

Which item did you find the most of? _____

Which item did you find the least of? _____

Name _____ Date _____

GRAPHING ACTIVITY

Find and graph the items listed. Then answer the questions below.

How many of each?

☐ 🍦   ☐ 🍿

☐ 🥨   ☐ 🌯

Which item did you find the most of? _____

Which item did you find the least of? _____

Name _____   Date _____

COMPLETE THE PATTERN

Look at the patterns below. Cut out the images at the bottom. Paste the image that comes next in each pattern.

Name _____   Date _____

COMPLETE THE PATTERN

Look at the patterns below. Cut out the images at the bottom. Paste the image that comes next in each pattern.

Name _____ Date _____

COMPLETE THE PATTERN

Look at the patterns below. Cut out the images at the bottom. Paste the image that comes next in each pattern.

Name _____   Date _____

COLORING ACTIVITY

Color the picture below.

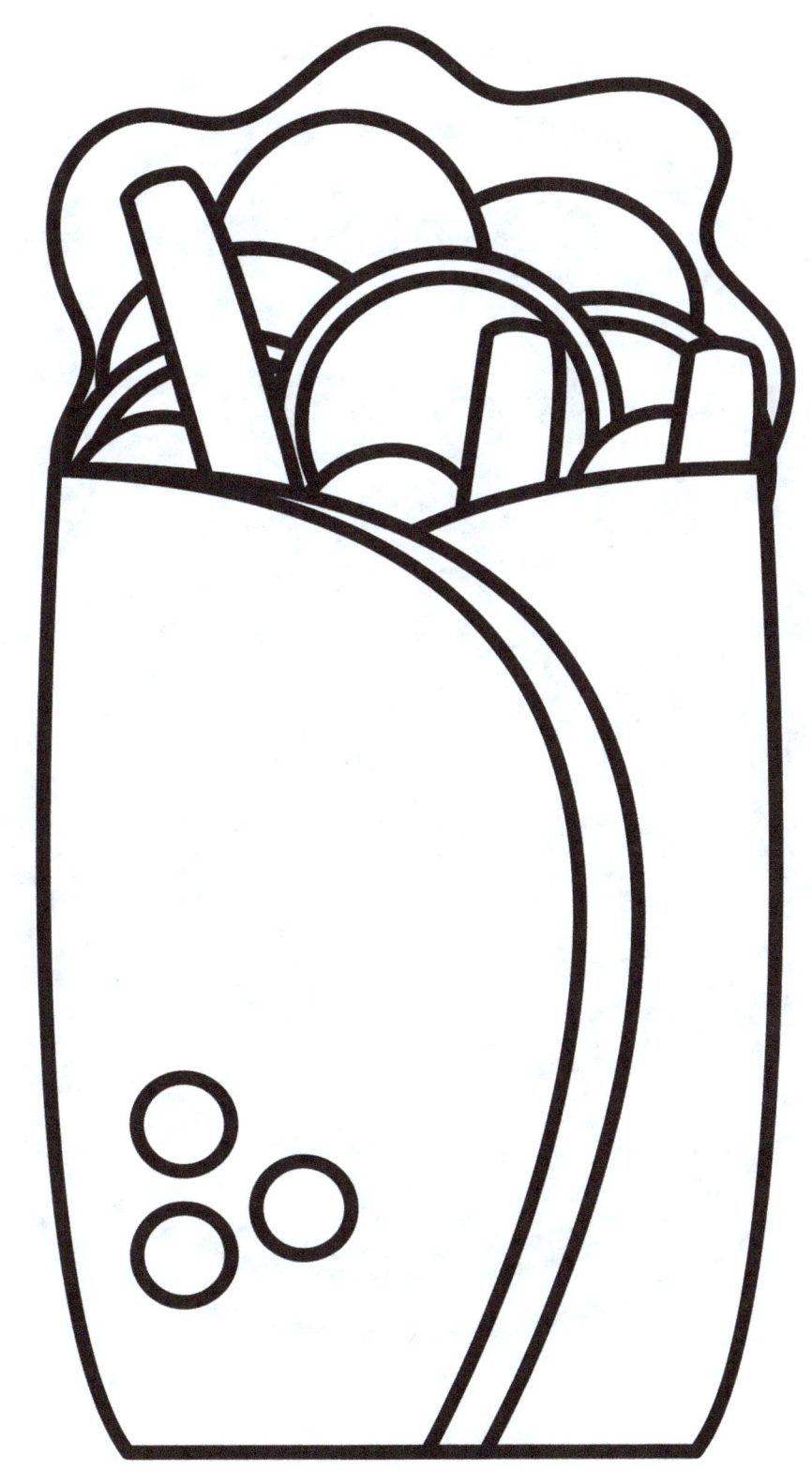

Name _____ Date _____

COLORING ACTIVITY

Color the picture below.

Name _____ Date _____

COLORING ACTIVITY

Color the picture below.

Name _____ Date _____

COLORING ACTIVITY

Color the picture below.